MW00479713

"May your coming year be filled with magic and dreams and good madness. I hope you read some fine books and kiss someone who thinks you're wonderful, and don't forget to make some art -- write or draw or build or sing or live as only you can. And I hope, somewhere in the next year, you surprise yourself."

-Neil Gaiman

on airplane mode

I can turn off and on so easily
dodging phone calls strategically
avoiding the places I should be
curating things that people see
of me

but I'm more than my own debris
so I'll descend back to reality
and consider myself lucky
when I'm 30,000 feet
in misery

on a lonely layover

Some days the anxiety of finding something to do in an unfamiliar city overwhelms me to the point of embracing Netflix and a hotel room with open arms— but I also find that going out alone recharges and resets me.

I love hearing about what people like to do in their favorite cities (everyone likes different places for different reasons)! This is my go-to jumpseat small talk.

I keep a note in my phone for every city, and when someone suggests something I write it down in case I ever find myself on a lonely layover.

Personally, I tend to gravitate towards independent bookstores, pretentious coffee shops, and record stores. I also try to walk everywhere in case I stumble upon interesting shops and sights along the way.

ideas 4 u:

Art museums
Murals
Hiking trails
Breweries/coffee roasters
Indoor/outdoor markets/antique malls
Tourist traps
Karaoke
Focus on your physical fitness
Start collecting something
Find the cultural neighborhoods (Little Italy's!
Chinatowns! Koreatowns! Etc!)
Become a Yelp superstar
Independent bookstores/cinema
(some cities have cult movie nights or show
movies in a park during the summer)

things to do in a coffee shop or in the wild:

Take language lessons during meals alone
Send postcards or handwritten letters
Podcast/blog/instagram/book club
Buy a Polaroid camera
Crochet/cross-stitch for a side hustle or gifts
Learn calligraphy
Become a beer or coffee snob
Read a book a week (I start one every Sunday)
Geocache
Write poetry or stories or your magnum opus

there is nothing more terrifying to me

TAXI

than a New York City cab ride

JFK

I let the words soak in when I'm feeling a little off the rails. It's hard being in charge of your own spiritual well-being.
Sometimes you just need people.

The loneliness of New York City is unraveling me

ATL
layover notes

Get out of downtown!

If you're looking for something fun to do with your crew and the weather is nice, take a cab to Krog Street Market and order a snack at one of the stalls. Grab ice cream from Jeni's and then head across the street to jump on the beltline to walk down to Ponce City Market.

After you're done exploring the inside of Ponce, head up to Skyline Park which is located on the roof. It's a little expensive, but worth it. Order a beer or boozey slushie and play a round of put-put/carnival type games with some of the best views of Atlanta.

My favorite restaurant in the whole city is Carroll Street Cafe. Pro-tip: On Mondays they do $5 tapas (flank steak is a must) and half off select bottles of wine. Tues-Thurs they offer half off tapas between 3-7.

LGA

Sometimes I get caught up in all the things
that I don't have. I feel it when my job takes me
to a faraway city and a lonely hotel room.
I feel it even more when I return to my cluttered
apartment in New York City that I share with
four other girls.

My friends are all getting married and having
happy fat babies, and I'm over here hoping to get
coffee-drunk by 9 am and not cry every time I
hear Julien Baker sing "Something".

It gets really dark in my heavy heart.

PDX

I'm tethered to the sound of your voice
on the other end of the telephone;
counting the hours and minutes and seconds
until we're both finally home.

on slam-clicking

Remember that you should never feel guilty for taking time to rest! Your body travels in and out of time zones and your sleep schedule is not normal

~but~

Please be mindful of how you utilize your alone time. If you spend too much time watching tv or endlessly scrolling on your phone, you're going to really feel the emptiness of this job.

Get out and live a little. Engage in something that improves your brain or fills your heart up.

Also going to throw this out there— I've made great memories tagging along with crews who I didn't feel like I had anything in common with while doing things I didn't really feel like doing.

Sometimes you don't realize how much you need human connection.

AMS

I'm tired on too much caffeine
jet-lagged and stuck between
adventures fueled by dramamine
or sticking to the same routine

As ridiculous as this sounds, stop listening to sad songs for a little while.

You put out what you put in.

If you have spotify, search for my
"Emotional Support" playlist.

Email me at eternallyoptimisticmail@gmail.com
to contribute your favorite songs about traveling
or getting happy.

AUS

haven't heard your voice in a year but
I won't complain
your new friends call you by a different name
ten years of secrets, won't spill 'em out loud
maybe you're alright but I'm full of doubt

I have to ask you this, just in case
could we make each other better people
or is it too late?
too late?
too late?
too late?
hey city slicker, is it too late?

"My heart is at ease knowing that what was meant for me will never miss me, and that what misses me was never meant for me."

-Iman al-Shafi'i

on sad days
how to throw a pity party:

step 1.
Find an album: something highly dramatic, that
you will only listen to when you're wallowing. I
suggest jazz, opera, or Hybrid Theory by
Linkin Park (lol). Play it as loudly as you can!

step 2.
Pick an activity to do while listening to that
album: take a bubble bath, bake some pizza rolls,
build a pillow fort and cry in it, do laundry, scrub
your house down, color your hair (don't tell your
hairstylist I suggested that), dance around
naked!

Most importantly:
feel whatever you need to feel.

step 3.
Choose a film: something you only bust out when you're feeling blue. Surround yourself with ice cream/snacks/beverages of choice and hunker down. Personal favorites include: Gone With the Wind, Casablanca, Amelie, and She's The Man ("DOES HE HAVE YOUR NUMBER? 1-800-BIOTCH?")

step 4.
Turn your phone on do not disturb mode (don't skip that part), rub your body down with some LUSH "Sleepy" lotion, put on the coziest pjs you own (or give yourself an excuse to buy some) and go to bed early.

I hope you wake up feeling new,
but it's okay if you don't.

when you have no idea what to do,
just keep recycling yourself

DTW
layover notes

Start by having breakfast at Parks and Rec Diner. Then, head over to the Detroit Institute of Arts— most notably there is a famous Diego Rivera mural you must see. The Museum of Contemporary Arts is *free* but please consider donating a small amount. John K. King Used & Rare Books is definitely on my list of top 3 bookstores in the entire world.

For hanging out, my first choice is midtown. If you need to get some work done, Great Lakes Coffee Roasting Company has a great vibe. Wander up and down those surrounding streets and you'll find more shops and breweries.

Dinner at Green Dot Stables or Slow's BBQ—worth the cab ride. Hangover/late night food at Honest John's.

Eastern Market has an incredible weekend farmer's market during the summertime. The electric atmosphere (the music, the people, the food, the smells, the shops nearby) makes it my favorite market in the entire United States of America. YES, I know what I said. I love Detroit!

CAK

Annie's awake and
afraid I'm gonna drown
drunk
and ripe from self-loathing
in her pink bathtub
at 26
but I guess
in my dumb head
I figured I was rehydrating
my broken body
with osmosis or some shit
so even if I
expelled out everything that
was swallowed tonight
I could just
open up the drain
and be made clean
by morning.

"Promise me you'll always remember:
you're braver than you believe,
and stronger than you seem,
and smarter than you think"

-A.A. Milne

tag me on IG @lasinlo
and/or send me your suggestions!
(I like local divey joints)

#MidwestBreakfastTour

CAK: Okay, I grew up in Akron so my opinion is biased. Go off the beaten path to Cuyahoga Falls. The Blue Door Cafe and Bakery
or Flury's Cafe
CLE: West Side Market Cafe
or Lucky's Cafe
CMH: Katalina's
DTW: Rose's Fine Food
or Parks & Rec Diner
FAR: BernBaum's
FSD: Josiah's
ICT: Doo-Dah Diner
IND: Good Morning Mama's
LIT: The Root Cafe
MCI: Opera House Coffee & Food Emporium
MSN: Johnson Public House
MSP: Victor's 1959 Cafe
OKC: Runway Cafe
OMA: Saddle Creek Breakfast Club
ORD: Pick Me Up Cafe
or Lula Cafe
PIT: Barb's Corner Kitchen
SDF: Please & Thank You
STL: Southwest Diner

BIL

It's the Fourth of July and I'm locked in my hotel room drinking decaf coffee in bed. I could probably rank hotel beds according to comfort all across the country if I sat down and thought about it, I mean, really thought about it. But instead, I'm thinking about all the sordid hotel beds you and I seem to find each other in. Wasn't it Leonard Cohen who sang, "and everything depends upon how near you sleep to me"? Damn, that's romantic.

"You may not control all the events that happen to you, but you can decide not to be reduced by them."

-Maya Angelou

ORD

memories are a curse when
you're treated unfair
but
I still look for your face in
every bar at O'Hare

on clarity

If you are seriously unhappy and nothing is
changing, it's time for some hard truths.

Give yourself a few hours at a coffee shop,
take a notebook, and NO MUSIC
(your mind needs to be clear).

Now the hard part: be *honest* with yourself
and jot things down if you need to organize your
thoughts.

What is going on in your life that is contributing
to your unhappiness?
Living situation? Personal relationships?
Work/life balance? Finances? Mental health?
What do you find yourself complaining about
the most?

What can you do to change this?
Come up with some ideas and how you could
realistically change the circumstances that are
effecting you.

Once you determine the roots of your unhappiness, start talking about your feelings to people you love and trust. I finally owned up to my depression on a trip to KEF with two of my best friends— we were sitting in a hot tub in the middle of nowhere with wine and stars and snow, and I confided in them about the sadness that was looming over every aspect of my life. Nothing changed in me right away, it was a process, but in that moment it was a relief to talk honestly about my feelings without judgement.

Look, I know sometimes the resolutions to our problems seem crazy and impossible to do, but I'm here to tell you that you are capable of anything.

You might be struggling with some serious stuff you can't even begin to describe, please remember I'm here to support you, and there are people in your life that support you, even if they aren't your family or close friends. Nobody really understands the hazards of this job quite like other flight attendants— open up to your crews over coffee or drinks— I've gotten some great advice and support that way.

Also remember, there is NO shame in seeking therapy with a trained professional.

"Let everything happen to you: beauty and terror. Just keep going. No feeling is final."

-Rainer Maria Rilke, Book of Hours

ATL

there is nothing a girl like me can't do
I could lose my cool
or get over someone like you

always got my city in the rear-view
all my houseplants are dyin'
do I treat them badly too?

"I believe depression is legitimate. But I also believe that if you don't: exercise, eat nutritious food, get sunlight, get enough sleep, consume positive material, surround yourself with support, then you aren't giving yourself a fighting chance."

-Jim Carrey

PIT
layover notes

(For a perfect Pittsburgh day,
be there on a Sunday—
everything I love is closed on Mondays)

Brunch at Zenith starts at 11, get there early
because it gets crowded, but you can meander
around the vintage shop while you wait for a
table. Disclaimer: it's a vegetarian restaurant,
but I promise it will blow your minds, trust me
on this one. Head over to the Mattress Factory
Museum and don't skip any of the buildings.
Then swing over to the Andy Warhol museum.
One of my crews and I managed to hit all three
spots before our pickup late that afternoon.
Y'all can do it.

if it's not Sunday:

Check the operating hours of Zenith/the
Mattress Factory/Warhol Museum, but if they
are open, you should 100% still go.
If not, you could always go see Randyland
or the Duquesne Incline.
At night, swing over to Hidden Harbor Tiki Bar
and take your crew!

decompression: when there is a loss of cabin pressure and a panel above your seat opens to reveal oxygen masks.

decompression: when I come home to my one-bedroom apartment in East Atlanta after days and days of small talk and hotel rooms. I'll turn on the record player, light the candles, and avoid my friends for the night because I

just need time

to be still.

LAX

does everyone alive in Los Angeles
have a disease
no one looks you in the eye when you
walk down the streets
I'm beginning to hate this whole city
and all the tall trees
small-talking with strangers in
uber backseats

In the movie "Katy Perry: Part of Me" there's footage of Katy having an emotional breakdown in her dressing room while thousands and thousands of people are waiting for her to take the stage in Brazil. She's crying so hard she's unable to speak, regardless, she still makes the decision to go on.

Then you see her... waiting to enter the stage, candy tits swirling, looking depressed af before she has to plaster a huge smile on her face for her crowd.

Some days you are going to feel just like Katy Perry did— and even though it might be difficult to stay positive when you don't have a net worth of $330 million to ease the pain, I'm putting good energy out into the universe for you and that's gotta be worth a least $2 million, right?

MIA

I stopped looking for emergency exits
the moment my life was cut in half
cleanly—
into you, and everything that ever came before

CLE
layover notes

Welcome to my wheelhouse.

If you're staying downtown and want to go out to eat somewhere fun with the crew, I highly recommend Barrio. Trust me on this one. East 4th is a little walking street nearby with restaurants and a coffee shop called Erie Island Coffee Company that I love. The Rock and Roll Hall of Fame is expensive but interesting.

Now, if you're down for some adventure, take a quick cab ride across the bridge to a neighborhood called Ohio City— this is where I spent 80% of my life when I lived in Cleveland. (Quick note: there are more breweries in Cleveland than you could possibly handle. If you like craft beer, you're literally going to be in heaven.)

The Plum,
Platform Brewery,
Great Lakes Brewing Company,
Nano Brew (great patio),
ABC Tavern (hipster dive bar),
Mitchell's Homemade Ice Cream,
Tabletop Board Game Cafe.

If it's nice out, walk down to Passenger's Cafe and take your beverages up to the roof of the Cleveland Hostel where you will find some of the best views of Downtown Cleveland.

The Hingetown neighborhood has a bar called Jukebox that serves pirogies and has a great jukebox, obviously. Rising Star Coffee Roasters is *amazing*, I highly recommend taking home some beans. If you don't enjoy coffee, Cleveland Tea Revival is right across the street.

a little out of the way, but so good:

Fat Cats—Fun fact, I used to bartend here before becoming an FA. Best happy hour in town, order many, many, many different things. I dream about this food.

Happy Dog— Hipster dive bar/music venue with build your own hot dog (has veggie dogs, dawgs)

Banter— Poutine and sausages and beer. Order food then pick a craft beer from the coolers in the other room. Also has fancy wine, I always leave with a bottle to use later as gifts. This is *THE* spot. Worth the cab ride.

MSY

you've been implanting bits and pieces of me
into your bones and into your body
like it or not
I still hear your voice in my head
while I'm trying to fall asleep
on and on ad nauseam
just like a skipping record I could
never turn over
and I keep listening
until my eyelids shutter up like
storm windows in New Orleans

on finding balance

If I make plans, there's a 65% chance that I'll follow through. It's not that I don't want to be there for my friends and family, but often times my tired body calls the shots.

On the other hand, when I put my work and sleep schedules ahead of everything else I feel like I'm runnin' on empty from the lack of love and social interactions I need to stay balanced.

I have to make a conscious effort to keep an equilibrium that makes me happy across the board.

a croissant:
flaky and
falls apart easily

~it me~

SFO(MO)

if I just don't pay attention to what you're doing
when I am not home,
and somehow ignore all the pictures you send
straight to my cellular phone,
or if I could only stop wasting time counting the
miles that I have flown,
maybe I would learn to not feel so lonely when I
am sleeping alone.

"Life's too short to wake up with regrets.
So love the people who treat you right,
forgive the ones who don't and
believe that everything happens for a reason.
If you get a chance, take it.
If it changes your life, let it.
Nobody said it'd be easy,
they just promised it would be worth it."

-Dr. Seuss

MDW

your words stuck like honey in the back of my
mind
i'm singing them back to you
in the bathroom
while I'm naked, brushing out my hair.
tonight i'm an arsonist lighting up your
selfishness for the very first time in
eight years or so
in the back of the cab and this hotel elevator.
you'll never find me exactly where you left me,
from Chicago to Cleveland
with tired eyes and
lips that taste of smoke and champagne.

on little things

I've realized lately that I am a mood sponge—
so susceptible to allowing how my crew is
behaving to seep into me.

If my crew brings negativity on board, it's gonna
bring me down. If they are contagiously upbeat,
(I'm gonna be annoyed at their perkiness but)
I'm also gonna feel good.

As a new hire, I was broke, depressed, overworked, and tired all the time—my old NYC roommate, Kaitlyn, puts me in the best mood by just existing, so we would often swap to work on each other's trips.

Those passengers got the very best version of me because we would just laugh and smile the whole time.

If I'm feeling emotionally drained from the people around me, I always try to swap to work a trip with someone who fills my heart up to the brim.
(Even if it's the crappiest trip of all time!)

top 5 layovers w/ Kaitlyn:

1. Two short layovers on a crappy 3-day trip: we rented a car, slept two hours, and then hiked up a ridiculous mountain in BZN to watch the sunrise. Then, we went to Western Cafe and ordered 3 full breakfasts to share. The next day we cried our way through The Lorraine Motel in MEM and grabbed some barbecue for lunch.

2. Thirty hour LAS layover: we got into our bathing suits and filled the tub up with bubbles, jammed to music, drank wine, and accidentally drowned Kaitlyn's phone. The next morning we walked (very hungover) to Taco Bell Cantina and got slushies.

3. Once we went grocery shopping and did a little meal prepping beforehand. It was actually a lot of fun seeing what we could come up with— some elaborate concoctions came out of that first class oven on that trip.

4. City Museum in STL was a BLAST. It's like an adult playground. We took so many photos. One of the best layovers I've ever had.

5. NYC layover— we had an amazing meal and then went to Madame Tussauds. It was expensive, but hilarious and memorable.

PIT

i'm a mess!
flying high
with enough emotional support gin
to fill your hollow heart

i'm a hypocrite!
so c'mere
this plane could crash from all the guilt
i've been carrying-on

no matter what breaks your biscoff
or pushes your call light
i'm on your side.

allison

p.s.

even on the darkest nights
your spark could light up every city—
from NYC to ATL to SEA to DTW

Made in the USA
Columbia, SC
27 September 2019